Look at Me

Written by Peggy DeLapp
Illustrated by Kate Flanagan

CELEBRATION PRESS
Pearson Learning Group

"Look at me," said the boy.
"I can run."

"Look at me," said the girl.
"I can slide."

"Look at me," said the boy.
"I can swing."

"Look at me," said the girl.
"I can skate."

"Look at me," said the boy.
"I can climb."

"Look at us.
We can jump rope,"
said the boy and the girl.